Matronalia

Matronalia

A. B. DILLON

thistledown press

Thistledown Press Ltd.
410 2nd Avenue North
Saskatoon, Saskatchewan, S7K 2C3
www.thistledownpress.com

Library and Archives Canada Cataloguing in Publication
Dillon, A. B., 1968–, author
Matronalia / A.B. Dillon.
Poems.
ISBN 978-1-77187-153-2 (softcover)
I. Title.
PS8607.I458M38 2018 C811'.6 C2018-901134-3

Cover photograph by Kimberley French
Author photo by Tom Walker
Cover and book design by Jackie Forrie
Printed and bound in Canada

Canada

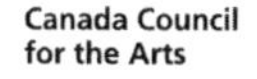

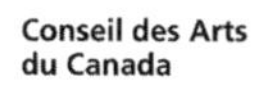

Thistledown Press gratefully acknowledges the financial assistance of the Canada Council for the Arts, the Saskatchewan Arts Board, and the Government of Canada for its publishing program.

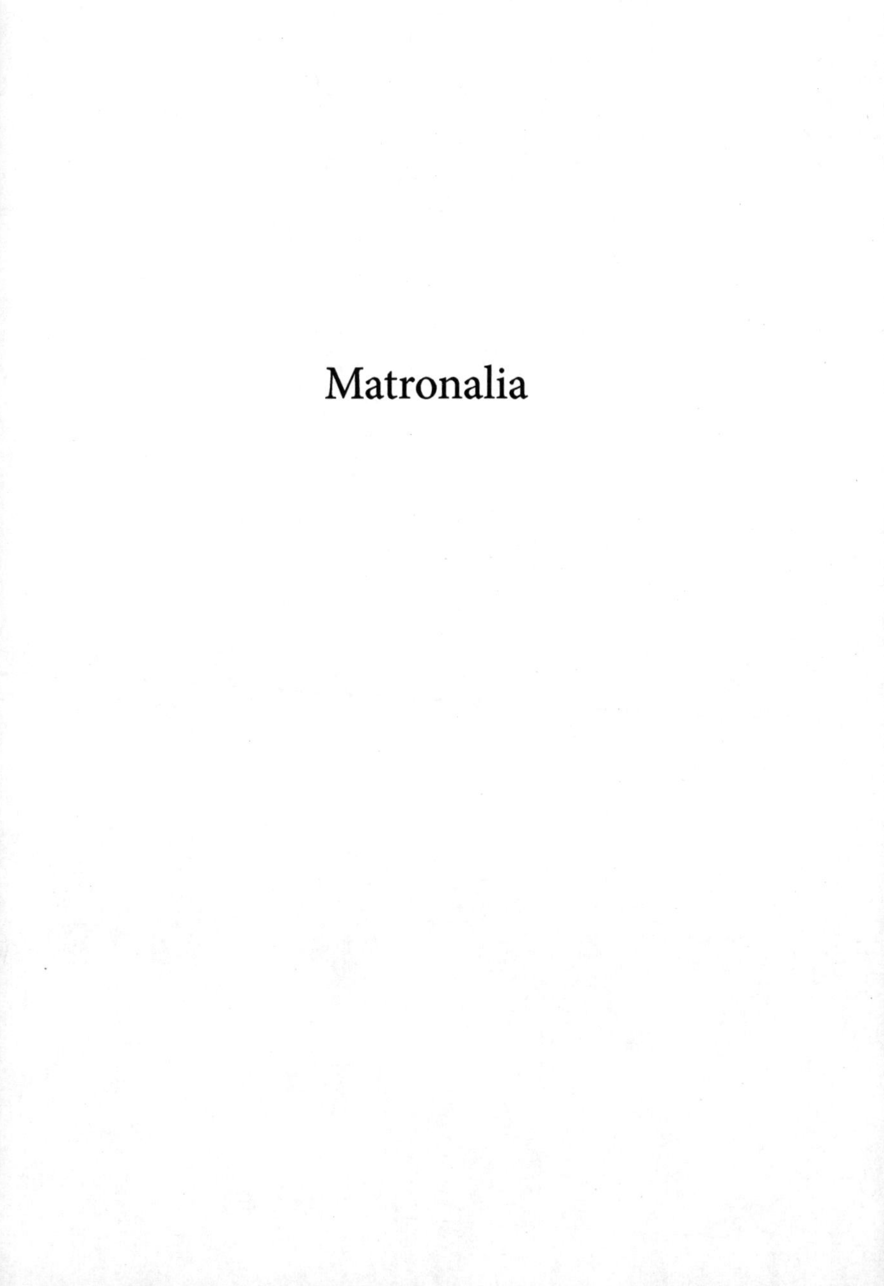

Matronalia

for Grace

Last night you said you felt a disconnection. You were not wrong.

The truth of it is that when you were born and my mother cried out It's a girl, my heart constricted. That's the awful, terrible, stone secret I have carried. You came by this Baltic love without having done a single thing. You were perfect.

The females in our family are incapable of loving each other with a soft heart.

We can love our sons, though.

My Girl, when you were born and she said It's a Girl,
I felt cursed, and immediately thereafter, I felt guilt.

So you see,
there were three things born that day,
and one thing that died.

You sensed it. Your sonar went into high alert as you suckled and studied the stricken face of your mother. (Female infant, green-eyed beauty, beseeching, beseeching.)

There was something missing in the milk. You felt a hunger that would not be satiated. I felt culpable, found out, afraid of your green eyes.

Once I rocked you too hard because you wouldn't stop screaming. Terrified, I set you down and walked away, as though you were a piece of crystal I touched and nearly broke.

I stood in the corner and screamed silently into the wallpaper. It smelled fusty. Everything about me was heavy and pendulous.
There was no part of me that I recognized.

Many days we stay inside. You play under the dining room table and I watch you from my spot on the sofa. You are deep into play, deep into the surface of the object in your hand, turning it and turning it again and again.

I am irrelevant to you. I am no longer functional as a thinking being. You have infected me with some sort of fever. I'm sure of it. There is a delirium. I blame the innocent.

The natural rhythms splinter.
None of the numbers are in the right order.
You have wandered into my ward
and infected me. I'm sure of it.
On the stairwell when I take you to your crib,
without saying it, you announce,
there is no way either of us is going to sleep.
You grab hold of my hair and pull.

You came upstairs to say
that you were sorry you were making parenting so difficult.
You said
you wished we
had more of a connection.
We grow ribs like hidden antlers (or coral) that causes
such constriction
around the heart,
it becomes impossible to breathe.

You came upstairs, to say,
and I couldn't speak properly.
It wasn't my fault.

And I didn't want to force it so hard that an inhuman sound bypassed one of the ribs in my throat and scared you or embarrassed me, or both, so I simply accepted your apology and sent you away. I stayed quiet. Just in case.

When you knew I lost the baby, you ran to get me a Band-Aid, you said for my heart, to fix it. And you brought me a napkin for my eyes. You were three.

I made a mistake that day, in calling her. Part of this disease is that you forget it's genetic. When I wailed into the phone about how violated I felt by the surgery, by all the strangers with their hands in me, removing the baby, she calcified and accused me of being dramatic. She didn't like it if anyone else's losses were bigger than her own.

Did I teach you to listen to your gut when I left him or did I teach you to give up?

Did I teach you to lean in to your passions? Because this might be the antidote, I'm not sure.

It might be a placebo.

In a moment of consuming sadness, I went back to a place that had once held a moment of great joy. I had hoped that my sadness would lift, but it didn't. I sat alone on the hill overlooking the river, and wept, and waited for things to shift.

There came to be a strange sound overhead, and when I looked up, I saw three black crows flying very close, hovering directly above me. They were waiting, too. I took it as a sign. We hover over ourselves, the more curious, the better. I try now to hover over these feelings. They become branches. Occasionally, I can land.

I used to make French braids in your flaxen hair when you
were little. At what time did I stop doing your hair?
I can't remember the exact time, and this causes me to panic.
When you were very little, I pulled your hair through my
fingers
to make French braids
as if doing calligraphy.

Now I am thinking
of lasts

the last time I drew your bath,
the last time I carried you
upstairs to bed,
the last time I brushed your teeth
for you,
the last time it was me
who tied your shoes.

You were removed from the party because you put your hand over the birthday girl's mouth to stop her from talking, and made her cry. She came running into the kitchen and sobbed in front of all the mothers whose eyes slid over to mine. You ran in like a dervish, grinning, not getting the judgment.

I forced you to apologize and took you home from the party. Thing is, she was a brat and a loudmouth, and I should have laughed it off in front of all those pinched bitches, maybe tousled your hair and teased you to take it easy on your little friends, wandered away and gotten myself an olive on a stick or another soft cocktail.

Mommy was afraid of raised eyebrows and silences.
Mommy was a scaredy-cat.

I loved that you put your hand where it didn't belong.

There was a time when we were walking home from your school. You were eight or so. Life had not taught you that you were a girl yet. You were still unmitigated, unaware, fully conscious potential. You walked along with a stick you'd found. Standing on the stone fence, you held your stick like a spear. You were a little Nemesis. You were a warrior.

I dreamed once that I lost you. I wandered into an antique store fascinated by lamps, trying this one and that when I sensed that you were not with me. I had forgotten you.

I ran screaming through the streets but could not find you. My chest exploded with canon fire fear and my brain crawled with biting ants of recrimination.

This could be my waking, daylight trance if I allowed it. As your mother, I am almost always just about to run screaming through the streets to find you. If I'm not careful to lock up my chest when I drive to work, it may explode. If I think of you making your way through the day like a pilgrim shielding a lit candle in a windstorm,

I aimed to teach you I would not rescue you, so no, I wasn't the mother who drove your forgotten homework over to school. I wasn't the mother who took you in because your alarm somehow didn't go off. Yes, you did walk in the inner city starting at the age of 9 and yes, you were encouraged to go two blocks to the neighbourhood park to play by yourself. No, I didn't make a play date for you to do this. No, I did not wander down to the park so you could play while I sat there. I never organized a mommy's group or participated in one. I never discussed potty training or time-outs or brand names.

You learned consequences early.
You dressed yourself like a rainbow.
You were not invited to many birthday parties.

You became like me.

I went to see a shaman and he told me that my spirit animal was a raven. Behind him on the wall was a plaque that had the phrase 'stay wild' painted on it. Wild was beaten out of us. Comportment, above all, knees clamped together, ankles crossed, hands folded in lap. No one discussed the wild between our legs.

You will not be robbed of your wild, of your native curiosity, of your feminine divine. You will not be mutilated. You shall stay.

Get lost in your wilderness, again and again. You are not Penelope waiting and weaving and undoing. You are Ulysses and your body is what you will navigate.

I remember the confessional. We had to tell the priests, or risk being unclean, you see? From the age of seven, they made us tell.

Secrets were dirty, even if they could keep you safe, like hidden pockets of air that can float you along this river.

My women, they lied, hiding their dime-store secrets under the laundry or in the china hutch or the closet in shoeboxes, places I didn't think to look. I thought if you lied, you forfeited God. I felt like an orphan among penitent nuns.

(Beware of women in cloisters with their chatelaines and their beads, their chanting and their knees on marble. You'd be safer with a man.)

I am many diaries, and I know where all my keys are, except a few. I check the locks regularly. I make my rounds.

There will come a time when you look at me with nothing but scorn.
You will think you know better.
You will turn on your heel and walk in a direction opposite to the one I took.
You will feel triumphant.

With each step you believe distances us, your confidence will grow, as will your loathing of me, in commensurate measure.
And you will walk forty years like this.

You will not know until it is far too late that you are walking directly toward me.

My mother sends me things in the mail as she gets ready to leave. She is shedding.

I won't be upset if, years from now, you re-gift whatever I send. Except, keep the linens and the Waterford. And keep my books. Remember to open one now and then, breathe deeply.

The leather gloves she used to wear, the ones that I slip on and pair with my jackets or handbags, those will be too small for you. You have long beautiful fingers, like Georgia O'Keeffe. I have the maternal curse — soon these hands will be just like hers and hers before her, knotted by arthritis.

Maybe it's a good thing you won't be able to wear them. Think of all the guilt on the inside.

Don't give them away, either, come to think of it. Do like I do sometimes, and interlace the fingers with your own.

Pretend.

She was not rigid with him. She doted, and the softness seemed to come from nowhere I recognised within her. He knew pliancy. I calibrated my worth like a dedicated auditor. I kept careful watch of the abacus.

She could attach only to one.

I can't blame her. It's an awful disease.

A man or a boy will want the right to your body. He will whittle you down, girl, whittle you down. Remember this- no one, no church, no man, no boy, nobody, not even me, has a right to your body. You alone navigate the terrain of your beautiful estate.
Wander and get lost, wander and get lost.
Get wonderfully lost.

We have buried two dogs and two cats now. You are fierce
about burials. You trip deeply into your rituals.

Luca used to sleep at the foot of your little bed. I told you,
when you were so very sad that she was leaving us,
that her presence near you, to guard you,
would always be there to sense, if only you would close your
eyes.
She is always. She would be joining the essence of dog spirit.
Canis Mundi.

Damn, if that dog didn't break my splintered coral heart.
She would not leave you.

Before she left me to nap or to sleep, she'd pull the string and the music box would play. It offered some measure of comfort.

My dear, I forget the melody.

You will want to know about sex. You will want to know what to do and when. I promise you, when you come home to tell me, I will not compare you to Mary Magdalene.

Or, if it pleases you more to keep this news to yourself, be unbowed in your silence.

You mustn't keep coming to me with your secrets to confess. You must learn to guard your secrets. If you allow one or two of them to fly out of your chest like those birds in that Tarkovsky film, you will lose them forever.

And he might kill some of them and pull their feathers, numbering each. When you argue, should he ever feel truly threatened, he could locate feather number thirty-seven, and wave it before your wide eyes. Or when you finally sleep, he might pull the covers down and drag a white feather along the length of your spine.

If you sneak into his study in the middle of the night and find more feathers, pinned and labelled, or stored in jars, run.

You are a diary with a broken lock.

On your sixteenth birthday, she told you that you should be careful about boys. She was all talk of milk and cows. I saw you fight to keep your face straight and your mouth closed, but you did manage to politely interject and for every evangelical point, you answered like a heretic in need of saving.

When I had her in the car alone with me, I asked her to stop talking to you like that. She said her female grandchildren were being taken advantage of. I asked if it ever occurred to her that they enjoyed the sex they were having? And that they were selecting mates of interest to them? When she looked broken, I stopped talking. Her neck torqued twisted spindled toward the window and she stopped speaking. The prairies rolled by her blank face like a scroll.

Only one of my lovers ever unlocked me.

I gave up all my keys voluntarily. I emptied the two pockets of my nightgown, the pockets of my robe. I found the ones I had put in the soles of all those old shoes and dumped them out on the table. I shook them out of the books. I removed them from the glass jars behind the spices. In the end, all the drawers were emptied. He even had the one I wore around my neck on a red string.

There were between us on the table a pile of assorted keys, of varying sizes, over which he ran his fingers, picking up this one or that, to turn over and examine. In the beginning he unlocked me skilfully, pairing this key for that lock,
and he read me,
pulling his eyes over my secret words until I shook like a starving dog.

He stopped trying to unlock me, after a time. He stood up from the table, took a fistful of my keys and left. Some things about me remain locked, against my will, you see?

Beware, girl. Feathers and keys, once released, lose their functionality. The bird cannot fly and the book will not open.

And how can a bird sing once it is unlocked?

I have forgotten which key is for what.

We are like feral cats. You have found your moon but I have
lost mine.
There are no tides for me. I am on a raft in a great black sea,
in my new moonless sky,
and I am lost.

My body betrays.

My skin turns to tissue paper and my face is someone else's.
I do not recognize this face and
my neck is a travesty.

Your body is lithe. You blossom, pink, peach, plum.
You are lit up by the moon, a warrior riding her tides,
supremely, monarchical.
You are unfolding petal by petal.

My eyes will have dimmed by your zenith,
cataract clouded,

In this way, you are my last sunset.

You came by this Baltic love without having done a single thing.
So you see, there were three things born that day, and one thing that died.
The truth of it is
that
when you were born
and my mother cried out It's
a Girl, you mewed
like a newborn kitten.

The females in our family carry this awful, terrible, stone secret.

I was asymptomatic until I had you.
I felt guilt.
It's a Girl, I felt
cursed.

The truth of it is

Pizzicato

A silence, just before.
It's just a space.

When you think of it, what you hear in a symphony is the movement of hands and heartbeats, and a great communion of breath. Think of all the hands that made the instruments, all the hands that have played those instruments. Think of the intermingling of passion and the reception of passion, of hope, of transcendence.

What are you hearing if not infinity?

There might come a time when you don't get to say "our", like
"This is our only coffee table book" or
"That reminds me of the time when our vacation took this strange turn."

You might be tempted to feel like a failure.

We tend not to recognize "mine" or "I" as valid, unless we speak of "my path" or "my journey". Those are allowed, the implication being the path includes both mate and progeny tripping along behind you, or in front.

You are surrounded, even if you walk in solitude.

Most of us are encouraged to feel worthy only in "our", the great Dia Meter, the mundus, the whole.

Try to forgive them for this.
Then try and forgive yourself.

Be a spear.

I floated in sorrow before I was born.
I was born a hungry, howling wolf.
You were born a mewling cat;
you were born
of the Baltic Sea.

I found a list you had written of things you thought I should have for Christmas. Among them, 'barets' for my hair, and old books to smell.

You knew me so well, in your eight-year-old loopy cursive.

You'd been watching like a silent hawk, or maybe I had opened one of my oldest books and had you bury your face in it like I do.

I can't remember.

I have set you adrift in a small paper boat countless times. I have set you adrift in a quiet river that I knew would take you away from me. I knew that in my silence, and in turning away, even slightly, in casting my gaze at some other horizon that did not include you, I was harming you. And yet,

I set you adrift without paddles or a life jacket or water to quench your thirst, without care packages or saran wrapped snacks or Cheerios in Tupperware.

You waited without rocking, because paper boats tear. You waited serenely, those green eyes fixed on the back of my neck, while I paced the bleak shore.

If you wept, you did not show it;
in your paper boat, like a swan you waited.

You will find yourself in the bathroom, after an innocent shower, trying to make sense of what you see. You won't notice your hips until you're about thirteen when you metamorphose into a house of mirrors version of yourself.

You will want to somehow constrict your waist to the smallest circumference, pulled taut with a good measure of determination. You will sacrifice breathing to achieve this feat.

Later (tomorrow, tomorrow)
you will not notice
how bound you have become.

You cried because you couldn't decide on how to complete a project for your high school art class. You were full of hesitation.

There was once a time when you approached anything you wanted to make with curious abandon. I don't know when that left you. I don't know when your brush hesitated over the page.

I tell you, this was the precise demarcation of the end of your innocence.
The rest is about the return.

Was I washing the dishes when your brush hesitated for the first time? Did you turn to tell me? Maybe I was looking out the window in that way that mothers do, wondering how it was I came to be standing there at all.

Try and find your women.

There are those who don't grow extra ribs or have their jaws lock in sinew or have tumbleweed hearts like us. They are like water that floods and replenishes.
They are keepers of the well,
they are mermaids,
they are fish.

When you were five, at liturgy for children, when asked to share at circle time, you stood up and explained how Hitler killed himself, but only after he forced his girlfriend to do it first. You put your index finger up to your temple and pulled your pretend trigger.

The children laughed, pointing fingers to temples, an innocent suicide squad in the church basement.

You were asked to
sit
down.

You will want to come home, like the waves call at the Cliffs of Moher. It will be a powerful pull. You will feel every porcupine compass needle point toward home so painfully they will pierce your tongue, bristle your throat, prickle your eyes as they twist heartward.

Let me say this, little one,
remember why you left.

Clench your little fists, filled as they are with marbles, and plant your feet.

Remember, there was a time
when you

I don't recall what your first word was;
I didn't chronicle your every victory.

There was one word, though.

You could alter my behaviour with it,
move me across the room like a pawn,
have me open the fridge or the cupboard,
wait in stillness,
make me hover,
have me scramble, start and stop.

A simple, powerful word.

More.

You were born the day before yesterday, in the year of the fish.
You shall be named Stella Maris, the anointed one.
(Those are stars that are your eyes.)

Remember this,
remember
you are the vast deep sea and the dome of the skies and yet,
neither of these can contain you.
(Those are pearls that are your eyes.)

And the squealing seagulls rejoice in their blanched aerial
vault,
as your hair wetly everyway hazes about this,
your porcelain visage.

You draw down the sun,
and you give birth to the moon.

And your petal feet,
like roses play.

Offer your divine pain as a prayer, and walk away singing.
It will have nothing to do with popping cherries.

Cut off all your hair at least once.
Let it fall to the ground;
walk away.
Learn to discard.

In Notre Dame, on Easter Sunday, I lit a candle for you.
The organ rattled my ribs, and there was a young couple who
kissed each other at the altar of **.
I had never seen anything like that,
lust in a cathedral.
It gave me more hope than any prayer ever did.

You were only about twelve months old. The sunlight in the kitchen found the tips of your eyelashes while you considered the piece of strawberry in your hand. With your eyelashes on fire, you were pure consciousness. You were an invitation.

This was another time that I wept. It wasn't for you or for me. I wept for the beauty of sunlight on your unknowing lashes, and because you didn't know what it meant to hold a strawberry. For that moment, neither did I.

The strain of it is
the cinching
an antiquated containment
of baleen, hook and eye,
and gathering at your iliac crest,
a torso quite contained.

And how good and safe and kind the incarceration
that cane and ivory and wood invite;

Ribs entombed by whalebone
prevents a hapless puncturing of the heart,
shrouds joy or delight just enough
to keep the breath shallow
and measured.

All that would be soft, held rigid,
as it should be, my dove, as it should,
for your own sake, mind —

Stick to the long line and hold steady to the bedpost,
let the pull of our women, let the confinement come, and oh,
(remember who you are)

Can't you hear them whisper it? Can't you feel the slide of the strings?

Amn't I to warn you
of the impossible freedom in such captivity?

Last night you made a joke about how I love the dog best. Her dogness sees my humanity. How can I not love the bestness of this?

In the everynight, when I am aloneness with her, I rest my cement head on her belly. She forgives my weight every time.

With dog, there are no extra ribs, and I never have to open my mouth.

When I was a little girl, she bought me maxi pads and told me not to touch them. She told me to put them in my closet because there might be a time soon when I would need them.

I did touch them, secretly, and mingled anticipation with shame and pride. And when I went, triumphantly, like a parade marshal, to tell her of my good dirty fortune, she grew extra ribs and her jaw set tight.

When we were in Paris, you wanted to rent bikes and ride
along the Seine. I regret that we didn't. I was purely afraid.
My bockety heart wouldn't sing.

I admired that you weren't afraid, not one iota.
You were an aria in a marble chamber.

In those moments, you were nothing like me and that was
a relief, like looking at the sculptures in the basement of the
Louvre,
standing still,
covered in plastic or gauze. Protected.

I was wondering, did I hold you enough? Did you know that I was there in the night? Do you know that I stand in the wheat field, always near you while you consider the sky?

You dressed yourself like Madeline for nearly a year. You were six. You insisted on white high knee socks and your navy hat and coat. You wore your hair in a pageboy.

Now you stumble at what to wear. You study yourself in the mirror, in this dress and that, upset with your thighs or your Grecian belly. In the end, you revert to an Iron Maiden t-shirt and jeans. This is not you. It's armour.

For every part in dismantling you, I set myself on a funeral pyre, again and again.

Lying on the floor, you studied my Georgia O'Keeffe book and decided that her paintings looked like vaginas. This caused you to smile, but not to giggle. I liked that about you.

When you said out loud these look like vaginas mom
I said you're right.
You smiled and turned the pages.

When you were nine, I took you to Vancouver to see the O'Keeffe exhibit. Your pinafore days were long behind you.

In the gallery, my jaw never locked once.
Maybe my heart was also soft, and maybe you could feel that?

There are images of you twirling in the rain, smearing your face with mud like a warrior, sitting on the pier. These flicker fadedly, fadedly, like dusty moth wings, splices, only fractions, mere seconds.

A mother is a recorder, a journal, an illimitable, constant aperture.
We are seers, voyeurs of the worst order.

You were about six when you learned of homelessness. You tried to puzzle it out at the dinner table in front of your grand-parents who took a harsh view, but yours was the compassionate truth of a child.

You decided to bake brownies and make Easter cards to hand out, so you loaded up your red wagon and set off.

The streets were nearly empty, except for two men.

One thanked you.
The other read your card and ripped it up.
He ate the brownie and walked away.
I picked up the pieces and put them in my pocket before you could see.

Inside the card you had written "I hope you find a home soon."

This ripped up my heart and scattered it to the four winds.

You will find yourself looking at your reflection in a mirror, maybe on a Thursday morning, at a fine resort hotel. You will not recognize yourself as you are, but perhaps you will only see your child self for a fleeting moment. There will come a squall of dread and remorse and even loathing, and you will feel tired. You will ask yourself haven't you done all the work already, to put this sad child to bed?

Ask her gently to

my heart constricted and stayed that way
when you were born
That's the awful, terrible, stone secret
and one thing that died
and my mother cried out
The truth of it
my girl

When did I get so careful?
When did it ever become about how clean the kitchen was?

You were such a little pagan at the park. I used to love watching your fearlessness on the swings. The higher you went, the more joyful you became. The higher you went, the more off the hook I was, the more admiration I had, the more hope I felt, that you, with almonds in your pockets, were not of this world.

I can see you are readying to leave me. You got your first job. You are saving for a school trip. You must pull away in small measures over time — it's a long birth for mothers and daughters, in waves, in fits, in small moments, you must leave me again and again, each time a little further.

I am both relieved and dismayed. I am both relieved and

We have survived this long with only minor dramas. I have carried you this long without an intruder to your body, or a squad of girls to pull you down into their riptide. The most trouble you've ever given me is a messy room or an unkind quip.

But I get this feeling — call it a premonition, like when you look up from a summer walk to see the sky has somehow become an angry dome, a sulking blue, and for a few moments, everything within me seizes, because this knowing storm is gathering, of your uncertain odyssey, and did I prepare you? Because, my God, the skies are pregnant and heavy with warning.

I wildly open as many red umbrellas as I can, because I must protect you, but my darling, each one that I open, blows away, again and again, flying up and away from me before I can thrust them into your clenched fist.

I was exactly thirteen years old before anyone asked me what I thought.

I sat across from a woman who hired me to babysit for her. She babbled about this and that, getting to know the new babysitter, and I found myself thoroughly engrossed, not only by her light-hearted musings, but that she had the audacity to direct her attention toward me in the first place.

When she paused, and asked me what I thought when she paused, mid-sentence, wondering when she said when she paused What do you think? blinkingly waitingly for me and that question, moreover her real curiosity about what I thought, that I might be a human with not only thoughts, but opinions, when she paused after asking me there was a thermogenesis a dawning a combustion so incredible I forgot my words and I was struck stricken stutteringly paused in wordlessness.

Do you know that despite myself, I tried to learn in a nanosecond what it was to have a thought, and to accept that I could have an opinion? It was like perhaps reacting to a possible accident when driving. I had been used to a certain road, you see, and suddenly, a fallow deer appeared before me and I had to swerve into the bracken and over some unknowable cliff. I had to lurch into reason.

She reached out her hand to touch my knee, apologizing Oh I'm so sorry, oh — my dear, I'm so sorry but all I could do was shake my head and choke on unrecognizable sounds gushing from my chest and out my throat, like I'd been exsanguinated.

It looked like when startled animals are released back into the wild, their unknown benefactor having raised the gate to a new reality. I hadn't perceived my confinement for thirteen years, but she released me into the tall green grass, the expanse of my mind. I am most convinced she never grew extra ribs or ever had lockjaw. There was certainly nothing like coral in her heart.

I
always
worry
about
the
horses.

In his rental house, there was a nest in the gable on the porch.
A baby bird fell out and on to the steps in front of you.

Where was I when your heart burst and you learned about

If I could, I would go back and stay in it, die in it slowly, to have saved you from this moment.

I cannot bear to think of the others I know nothing about, when you were falling out of the nest I had built and abandoned.

When you stand in the tide up to your ankles, the receding
water makes you feel like you're moving, that you will be
pulled into the ocean and swallowed up whole.

Singing joy or thirsty sorrow
are like this.

A lover may make you feel this way, may make you feel
that you are pulling away from yourself in a chilling ebb that
leaves you off balance, careening and divested.

Dig your toes in to the wet sand.
After the heavingly wave,
and the beckoning pull,
look carefully for what the water leaves at your feet.

When you were about three we were at the park. Another mom didn't like how you were playing with her child and got to you before I did. She grabbed your arm and raised her voice. You were startled but not entirely affected. You moved on to play with someone else.

I have often thought of the red marks this woman left on your little arm, a scarlet imprint of each of her angry fingers.

My mistake was in being a few steps too far away.
My fear is that I will always be a few steps too far away.

I had such a beautiful dream this morning. We had bought a new house. It was old and solid and full of character. There were secret rooms and fireplaces, and the doors were sturdy — heavy like final statements. I felt elated. I felt relieved for us that we had found such a stunning mansion, and that we would be residing. We had landed. I had a sense that we were all going to be fine. It was one of those dreams that I knew I was having, and that I didn't want to wake up from. As I began to surface, I became aware of the cool breeze off the river kissing my forehead. I heard three geese laughing as they flew by my open window.

I used to surround you in a circle of books. I'd stand the books open so you'd have a book fort around you, a word moat, a chasm. This, you loved. It kept you occupied for hours. This was your enchanted ring, and you were careful to put each book back once you'd read it.

Vastly gone, gone away deeply, surrounded and subsumed,
delightedly you disappeared.
Gone away was my girl.

It was a holier place than any cathedral.

Do not believe in a man of God;
Believe in the woman behind the deli counter.

When in Paris, I took you to Shakespeare & Co.
You curled up next to a cat.
And then I spied it, slightly there, like a blush or a bruise, the ancestral melancholy
despite the beauty of the place. I saw it. Longing. Sadness. Ennui.

A great drowsy need awakened and stretched through you.

We could hear the cathedral bells trip through the open window,
and yet, you stayed curled up by cat, your green eyes almost yellow, like hers.

If you are ever missing me, truly, go to Tofino, to Cox Bay
Find the biggest log on the beach
Stand on that log and watch the flame of sunset extinguish,
listen to La Boheme.
My darling, I was there.

Beside me, on the left, there appeared a large dog,
and his such sweet face was so and
there was a plunging feeling in my chest
a kind of golden radiating pain
that caused me that consumed and there was
such a thrum such like a spear that
and to have pulled it out would have meant
that one could not be content
with anything but the feeling of

the surf winds dried my ecstatic tears before they had a chance
to fall, except one.

One wet the sand.

You may find yourself standing in a Sobeys in the deli section during your fifteen-minute lunch break. Glen Campbell's "Rhinestone Cowboy" will be playing over the loudspeaker.

You will not know how you ended up standing there, in a Sobeys in a small town. This was not your plan. You will be unable to choose between the day old quiche and the spinach dip.

People will move through their tasks all around you, the busy mother with her young boy in tow, the hair-netted woman behind the deli counter, the construction worker buying wings and fries. The man who runs the meat department.

The man with a clipboard.

All are moving through space and time.
You will stand still, unable to decide.

Forgive me.

When I knew I was pregnant with you, I stood naked in front of the mirror. My body looked the same and yet it wasn't. I was doubling. I was hosting, twinning, dividing. I was multiplying. I had joined the great murmuration.

In that old house, the bathroom had a door that opened on to a large balcony. I opened this door wide and climbed into the bathtub, where I floated, considering my body, considering you, and occasionally, the languid trance of the poplars and prairie grasses just beyond the open door.

I was returning to the waters. And in this endless swell, you were an echo I strained to hear. I was, after all, only the conduit, finally a vessel worthy of minor miracles.

I was not unlike Ophelia.

There are the videos or photographs of mothers and daughters laughing while cooking together in the kitchen.

I have no idea how to do this. My jaw sets and I measure tension like hot grains of sand into my chest while you stand there and look at me.

We are uncomfortable in the kitchen. There is no ease of movement and small talk and warmth. We resort to cooking or baking alone, although I did show you how to make Monica's pastry.

You were upset that I assembled the pie without you, but it felt so maudlin to me, so fake and made up this saccharine idea that we should commune in the kitchen somehow.

All my life I accumulated. I stockpiled. Now I am editing, removing, giving away, donating, clearing out, erasing, venerating. The other day, I saw a single pink peony in a brown glass jar and I thought to myself this, this is all there is. If only I had sat down at the kitchen table and climbed into a pink peony. If only I had kept the cupboards bare. If only I had guarded my heart and kept it empty as a sepia bottle, I could have heard the ocean.

You are married to the moon.
Remember.

During the worst of it, when things were falling apart, you were about ten years old. That's when the trouble with sleeping began, and that's when you told me that your scalp hurt. I noticed your fingers probing your scalp, when you were watching tv or looking out the window, rooting around for some cause to discomfort.

You asked me to check one day why this could be so, and I looked, parting your hair this way and that.

I don't see anything, I said.

Years later, from a very far away shore, a confession — you had been pulling it out yourself, strand by strand.

I had been looking in the wrong place.
I should have been searching your broken heart.

I have to brace myself for holding you. This is part of the pathology. Involuntary flinching.

When you have this disease, understand it is progressive. I wasn't this bad when you were little. Calcification was minor — hardly noticeable even, just a slight tremor of the heart, a hardening that no one could see, and possibly that you couldn't feel.

Now that you are taller than me, now that you need me more, in those seconds before you rest your head on my raven shoulder and lean your weight on these hollow bones, before you wrap your engulfing arms around me, I leave my body. I've tried to plant my feet. I've tried to breathe into remaining, but I vault. I morph. The extra ribs splinter across my guts like ice fractures.

It sounds like when a hapless bird is startled. It sounds like a cacophony of hurried wings. And I imagine, while you hang there, it must be like hugging an unfinished sculpture.

I watch you calculate the ease with which I hold your brother. This ossification of my heart is my own fault. I see my Medusa reflection. I do it to myself.

Baby girl, you'd need to be a jackhammer to pulverize this.

You asked me why no one has dated you and if you will ever get to go on a date in high school. I said yes, yes, of course you will have dates in high school. I told you to go back to your natural hair colour. You asked me if your hair colour was why you had not had a date. I didn't know how to fix this silence. I said yes, maybe, in part? And I did exactly what I never wanted to do. I had us both focus on your looks. I did the same to you as they did to me — I made it about your hair.

You went downstairs to cry. My jaw reset itself and I could feel new ribs forming. One dug into my gut and pierced my heart like a cold nail. I let it.

Somehow I will have to find something heavy enough to put on my chest to force the words out between my teeth. I decide that I will push this out — "It is never about your looks."

You will agree with me because I taught you to be respectful and you're scared of me and my Baltic love. But you'll think of this moment every time you dye your hair, maybe even when you are dyeing the grey out. You will remember the moment when your mother took something else away from you.

I spent the next few hours bending sideways into the pain until I heard it crack.

Once we all stayed at a place called Point No Point.

I had accrued by then many, countless alone hours with you. When you have this disease, spending too much time in an ossified state can be deadly. He left again, to go riding on his Italian road bike, and there we were, trapped in a beautiful cabin at a point with no point.

When he got back several hours later, it was my time. I went up to the main house to do my writing but nothing would come. It had been a few years of being blocked (the disease had moved to my hands and my brain had become an empty hive). I sat there, paralyzed and needing my words, but none emerged.

I saw where you had dragged your tiny finger across the windowpane the day before. You had left a track, a smudge, a finger painting with no paint. And suddenly, I missed you, like you had died or been kidnapped or somehow had left the earth, and then the idea of scratching words on a page became pointless too, because all I wanted was to bury my face in your neck.

Part of this disease is that you will feel completely normal, then out of ether, out of dreamscape or pure thought, it will come. There will be no extra ribs yet, or sinew that wraps like barbed wire around the jaw. There will simply be a distressing lack of energy. You will feel tired and think it will help to lie down. You lie down. It will not help, so you think you might feel better if you stay where you are. An hour will become three and you will feel worse. There will be weeping for no reason. You will realize you are in a burning house except nothing is on fire, but perhaps your brain cells or your soul. You will know you should get up and run because the house is on fire, but you cannot. You will stay prone and inert. You will think it would be better to not live like this, then you will think maybe if you keep lying down, it will pass. You will not eat. Your children will note that you are still in your housecoat. They will ask if you are okay. Lying to them will be hard, but you will. They will secretly not believe you. They will feel heavy as stones, and cold, like the shores of a river at dawn.

Years of waiting
for the fine bone china teacup
to break.

I have been told that I have two voices — one for you and one for your brother. When you have this disease, you speak in tongues. The best way I can speak to you is in words on a page. It's the safest for me, because you see, there is no sound and nothing seizes but my heart.

Out of all the places we could have gone, you wanted to go back to the bookshop, to find your special spot and climb in and lie down. You didn't even really want to read.

You wanted to commune with your own kind —
an ancient and indifferent feline,
bits of paper from strangers tacked to a message board,
the warm sunkissed dust like talcum on the skin,
the creak of tired floorboards, a sad excuse for a sofa, and books.

And the boy who played a slightly out of tune piano in the other room.

You might find yourself alone for a number of years, call it a kind of widowhood. You might feel married to a ghost.

The best advice I can give you is to sleep in the middle of your bed. Make sure you always keep your own chambers. Let him keep his own company, too. Visit when you feel the compulsion. Lock your door if you want. At least have the choice. That way, you will never grow used to a warm body percolating next to yours. Your cheek won't become dependent on finding solace upon a beating heart.

Better to turn over and clutch a feather pillow in the night. Pillows conform. Pillows warm, eventually.

If you feel the need for something cool, sleep with a man, but if it's safety you're after, better to just turn the pillow over.

When I tell you to heed my warnings, or when I offer you advice, I am always hoping for you to disagree. You came into this world complete.

For every single time I have deconstructed your confidence
(which I have done with a glance or a raised eyebrow)
I have felt like a felon.

I've been a merciless judge.

The truth of it is
I felt guilt

I was asymptomatic until I had you.
So you see,

love without having done a single thing

newborn terrible,

stone

secret

and my mother cried

What I have done is turn you into my mirror. I have seen my own reflection in you.
What an error, what travesty to have reduced you this way.

Could we not wander down to the lake together, some moonfilled ivory night, and look at our reflections? Dare I ask you to join me?

We could float our thousands of paper lantern thoughts into the darkness,
watch their twins be born in the sky.

I was told by a love that he and his friend waited for me to enter the lecture hall at university. When I walked in they said the Ice Queen had arrived.

My gone away love, the one who took my keys, he said I was a delicate orchid.

My lost husband said I was a shark, that if I didn't keep moving forward I would die. A shark is a killing machine, you know.
(That is what being a wife did to me.)

My darling, I wanted so badly to believe in orchids.

The feeling of the tip of her nail file
under my five-year-old nails,
and her telling me it was to get the germs out.

Not knowing what germs were, I asked.
Like worms, she said, only you can't see them.

Thereafter, always feeling unclean,
and afraid of my fingers.

When you were a baby,
I took you to the front yard
and let you play in the garden dirt on purpose.

It was a wartime victory.

Her lipstick was always perfect. She was the kind of woman whose handbag matched her shoes, and her leather gloves matched her handbag. She wore white gloves to mass, every Sunday. She was a terrible beauty, you see, and that made it worse, because it was all anyone ever expected. I swore I wouldn't be like her, but when I turned forty I spent a thousand dollars on a handbag. I line up my shoes like good soldiers, and as for my lips? They will always be blood red.

I confess that my anger has been misplaced. It's part of this disease, these bursts of rage against nothing. I never thought missing lids for Tupperware would bring me down.
I never thought the sputter of another dying light bulb would defeat me.

I wish I had been one of those boastful mothers who stood in the playground and folded origami shapes out of all your singular talents. I wish I could have been one of those mothers who showed off your 1,000 cranes, but I can't stand in circles, and when it comes to you, my dear, I'm a hoarder.

For instance, I cannot think of a single time when we just twirled together or when I might have touched your nose with my index finger in full approval of something silly you may have done. And that makes me wonder, was

There is a rage in me that does not belong to you, but you ignite it. You ask for my opinion about something innocuous. I feel a surge of indignant skin prickling chest blowing rampage. Then comes the mudslide of remorse. I want to apologize, I know I should apologize, but I sit in it, like being sent to the corner, I sit in it. There are no extra ribs and my jaw does not lock, and I find this curious, this new symptomology.

You are the patroness of the harvest,
Goddess of the underworld and of the sun.
Go to Leinster and stand on your hill.
You are Grainne.
Remember who you are,
especially while standing at the bus stop,
or in a bar, near a church
or in the line up at Walmart.

When you were little, you asked me to call you Cherry Blossom. I have only managed to force this pet name through my rib filled throat a few times. It doesn't sound beautiful when I say it. It sounds reedy. I feel like a grasshopper.

We could one day go to Japan in April, and wander under the slowly everywhere falling pink petals. I could walk with you, and my heart would sound like a hollow flute, even if you could not hear it. I could watch your perfect upturned face.

A friend told me that her father made her a coffee every morning and covered it with a piece of toast to keep both warm. I took to making you tea and bringing it to you on a tray.
You were very little, maybe eleven or twelve when I started doing this.

One of the problems with this disease is you can't seem to do anything for very long. You can't sustain. There are a certain number of times you can perform an act, and that number is elusive.

You are the neighbourhood flower thief. Since you were little, you've been coming home with stolen blossoms in your fists. You have an uncanny ability to make just the right arrangement. You have left little bouquets in my port glasses or my parfait glasses, on the windowsill or on the table. I have asked you repeatedly to stop, admonished you gently to stop, but this kleptomania has endured. You're like a cat with a kill on the doorstep — no guilt, simply green eyed presiding.

When I see another arrangement, it's like you've gone out for a walk three hundred years ago, when there were no chain link fences and flowers were free. I find it astonishing.

The things I have taught you to do — to make proper tea, to paint, to write a well-crafted sentence, to bleach your whites, to cook, to bake, to defend yourself, to travel, to dare . . . in all these you are superior to me. You have surpassed me and inch toward vistas I have never seen. In this way, I approach some semblance of what must be pride, or to be more specific, my darling, it's more like awe.

Part of this disease is that being broken, you see all the broken things. Every little broken thing (the door lock, the light bulb, the table, the lamp, the picture frame) is added to the heap of broken things that are in your charge to fix. And you simply cannot fix them all. You live in those first few moments after a long war, when you scan the horizon and see decimation. And you wonder how on earth you will crawl out from under this pile of destruction, until it dawns on you that out of everything, you are broken the most.

I had been conscripted. I didn't know I was fighting a losing battle.

If only I had raised every single white flag I could find. For every thought of defeat, I could have simply raised a white flag and stood out on the battlefield.

I could have released ten thousand doves.

There was a time
when all my careful consideration
went into selecting plants for the window boxes.

And yet, she gave me such precious things. She gave me all her gloves and silk scarves and she gave me jewellery she loved. She gave me her father's eyeglasses, my father's medals, my grandmother's rosary beads, my father's vases. She gave me letters they had written to each other, from over the sea when everyone was ruddy faced and afraid. She gave me my grandmother's shoes and brooches and she gave me the mantel clock from my grandparents' wedding.

You will see me carefully tending to these, my own odd trove, this garden of loved things.

Maybe these acts of giving were her antidotes.
In many ways, she was a selfless pietist.

I am not sure how many times I brought you tea. I wish I could say thousands. I wish you would be able to say something like *My mother brought me tea and toast on a silver tray every single morning.*

I'm certain you won't remember the handful of times I did. I am a handful of times mother, in almost every way.

When I was a child at school, during inclement weather, we were corralled into the library where we were shown a film on the projector. This is when I watched The Happy Prince. The singing of the little swallow who was determined to fly away to Egypt but never did, and the moment when the prince's jewel eyes were plucked out sent surges of such ecstatic pain through my tiny heart I scarce thought I would survive it.

I wanted to be the little swallow. I wanted the Happy Prince to love me. I was the poor girl who needed bits of gold.

I bought a rare edition of this book from John K King's bookstore in Detroit. I could never finish the story without crying, not once. I read it to you as often as we could both bear it.

I'm always flying away to Egypt.

Lament if you must,
accept the stone walls
and open fields of your heart.
Do not fight the grit of its beating.

Turn your face upward
to the rain.

At the foot of the David,
on the Pont des Arts,
in the Caravaggio room,
on the Ponte Vecchio,
walking over the River Liffey,
in the great library at Trinity,
at the Bridge of Sighs,
beside the river,
on the log at Cox Bay,
at the Sobeys unable to decide,

when I have long since left,
you will still find me here.

You were bold, and this angered him, so instead of giving you the flowers he had bought for you, he threw them in the garbage. Mark me, buy flowers for yourself at least once a month. Your heart is a rose that belongs to no one but you. Besides, who wants Safeway carnations when behind your ribs peonies flourish, and the linnets sing fresh and freely?

Go to art when you are lost, my darling.
Stand before something that breaks you.

When the worst of it was happening, I couldn't cook. My heart had gone out of the kitchen. I was in a wilderness and could not find my way back to tend the fire.

It was a Sunday.
I cooked a roast the way you liked, and you were overjoyed.
You said Oh Mama, can this be your goal?

I had been staring off into some bleak space, two unblinking sepia eyes, while the food spoiled on the counter. You had agendas and reminders and lists. You had been marching off to school in your own wilderness, with a sore scalp and a broken heart.

I made it my goal, on a Sunday.

You yearn for your gone away father the way I yearned for mine. At the beginning, before I had you, I vowed the you to come would never scavenge like me. And then I set about waiting for you, confidently, even smugly, certain that your belly and heart would always be full.

But at night, you with your cool pillow and me with mine, in this silence that blankets us, we both hunger for dried flesh on bone.

When you were nine, you auditioned for a choir. I did your hair in long spirals, which hung down your brown as berry skin.

I led you, and you followed, which crushed me more than you'll know, that you followed such a lost Sherpa as me, but you did it, serenely and innocently.

Darling one, when you sang, you vaulted me so high I came out of my coral shell and became flesh, soft, vital, assaulted upon hearing you. It was like being stung by one hundred thousand bees, the internal hum of it, the burning of my skin, the ancestral echo alive in you.

You were so full of the truth,
you led me up the mountain.

Nothing would please me better than if you were to

I release you from ever having to search my face before you leap.
Does the cherry blossom seek permission?

There was a time
when you were very little
everything felt calm
and green
with possibility.

my heart constricted
That's the awful, terrible
Baltic love

You were perfect.

there   were   three   things.

When you were in dancing lessons, or when you were skating, I could dress you perfectly. I could do your hair and makeup. But when it was your turn to perform, inwardly I was a twisted pile of sun bleached elk antlers. My face was a brick.

I wished for my face to be a vase of white daisies, and for my heart to be a soaking sponge, and for my smile to be full of light — and I wished I could throw my arms open, and that you would run to me as freely as the tide rushes the shore.

Your lovers will essay the cartography of your body.
They will not be able to chart you, though they will try.
Allow them this futility. It's the disorientation of love.

Have I sentenced us both to my mendicant ways?
It's just that when you really think about it,

Women who can rend a chicken's neck. Women who can break things because it means they put an end to misery. These are the ones to model yourself after.

I should have pulled over when I saw the seagull out on Granville Street with a broken wing, waiting in terror to be hit, but I hesitated and did not rescue, so how can I possibly save you from the likes of me?

You came home the other day fully light. A boy
extended his arm to you. You are beginning to feel seen.
Now I find myself wishing you were playing in the
sandbox, considering the sensation of wet sand on your
skin, not caring to be seen, only seeing
the red lit up shovel in your impossibly small hand.

Do you remember that time when a dragonfly became trapped in the hallway tower? It droned toward the windows in a frenzy, forsaken by faulty navigation of the crashing possibility of sky.

I thought myself a Joan of Arc. I thought I'd rush in and rescue, but every time it came near me in fanatical azure obfuscation, I shrieked and ran like a terrified child.

It was you who saved the dragonfly.

A boy once told me that he'd written our names on a lock
and secured it at the Ponte Vecchio.

I didn't trust this was so.
When I returned, I searched for it.

When it comes to locks and love,
when it comes to bridges, remember that you should always

I like her best when she swears and laughs. I like her best when she is playful. I have seen her play ping pong exactly one time in 48 years. I have seen her swim cautiously, like a starlet, not wishing to disturb her hair, maybe when I was eleven.

What would it have been like if she had run off the dock and into the cold lake whooping like a madwoman, maybe even pulling me in with her? How could I have come to know her if she had gone jogging or ridden a bike or clapped about winning a board game?

When I came home from a trip to Montreal, she said *Look, I vacuumed for your return*, but I don't remember running into her open arms with abandon. Homecoming meant cleanliness and order. Abandon was never an option.

I knew her from her crossed legs, her Matinee Extra Milds and Sanka coffee, her and L'air du Temps that preceded her or lingered after she left, the books open on her lap, and how she would look up and out the window, considering. I knew her mood from how the pages turned, or from the slow exhalation of smoke toward the ceiling. I knew her from the thud of the dinner plate before me, and the silence that followed after.

Rather,

when I am painting and you wander in, you consider the palette and perhaps listen to how the boar's hair scratches the canvas, and I allow it. I know you are learning, absorbing, musing. I used to watch my father paint thusly, and would not make a sound. But you see, when he was painting, I was invisible, and when I was invisible, I could breathe.

I assembled the pie without you so I could breathe.

We are not made for the kitchen, you and I.
We are en plein air.

When my grandmother lost her babies,
when, without her husband,
she took her daughters to the countryside during the war,
when she served tea to the soldier
and the cup clattered in the saucer because his nerves were that bad,
when she sat up and sewed
while the mantel clock chimed and all were sleeping,
these are the jewels I pass on to you.
I tell you these stories as they were told to me.
We unearth them and turn them over in our hands
careful for the details.
These are our runes.

I was taught in school to be a selfless person of servitude, to reside behind the thick walls of martyrdom, to wash filthy feet in penance, to turn the other cheek.

Be selfish, my girl, be a starling rogue. Fly inside each experience and let that serve you. Hurry over these walls, out into the meadow, above the rabble. Let me see the skies reflecting on the fierce green marble of your eye.

Never turn the other cheek.
Turn on your heel, should anyone dare

Leave the martyrdom to me.

Know that you are anointed. You are the anointed one, the grain Goddess,
the giver of life. And for goodness sakes, stop slouching like that.

When you were turning two-years-old, I did your hair in piggy tails with white daisy elastics. You were in your pink and white gingham cotton dress. You were a gentle little thing, with a gentle little smile and a wide open unprotected heart.

I tried to make you a castle cake. Everyone had the good sense to say nothing. It was a disaster and I was mortified. Why did I fuss? Why did I put myself through such tests?

Why didn't I just wrap my arms around you and go lie down in the tall grass? We could have puzzled at the sky instead, your two-year-old sky.

I never found it.

There was the first time
you became aware of me.

A consideration passed over your face,
something of an awakening,
and you reached out your honest hand,
touched my cheek and smiled.

I wonder how many ribs would I grow
if you tried something as honest now?

She bent the metal bedframe pulling on it while she laboured. Twelve times she laboured. And then they churched her because she was unclean. Forty days she was unclean, twelve times.

You come from this kind of strength. Please remember, of all things, the very last thing you are is unclean. The very first thing you are is sublime. Neither of these states of being has anything to do with the number forty, a man-made number for man-made sins.

I know now that every single time when you asked me, I should have said,

Yes.

And there are moments like this morning when I feel such a profound sense of forgiveness for her that my heart unearths and the coral falls away. My ribs feel as though they are open white lilies and my throat and jaw swan peacefully.

And when she says she's lit a novena candle for me at the altar of Our Lady, why do I weep skeptical tears?

I hope when you consider me, when I inhabit my crone self, you will arrive at this compassion, one day, however unexpected, like when a crow calmly descends and cries out, breaking the silence with its onyx zealotry.

After I bashed the tin bowl against the sink, I went out and bought pretty lights for the back garden. You had left me another pile of dirty dishes, and I saw this as a kind of mutiny. There are no surfaces that remain peaceful in this house. Last night, as I clobbered the bowl into submission, I swear, I never felt closer to my mother. Servitude makes lunatics of us all; but maybe the promise of fireflies in the garden isn't

I wandered in to Notre Dame during high mass. It was Easter Sunday, but I had quite forgotten. I was half asleep from the travel.

The organ played, I think it was Bach. My darling the organ was so loud it verily though I walked through so many shadows, an instant penitent I was, all my gone away people were with me, even the baby I lost, and the organ was so full-mouthed that I was heartily sorry for having offended thee and I can't tell you what it was like to have that music violate my soul. There was an impossibility of extra ribs in that space no matter how advanced the disease, you see? And all my people seen and unseen, all my thoughts and all my words, in what I had done, in what I had failed to do, they were praying for me to the Lord our God, and I didn't care. I just stood there, looking at the Rose window, and my ribs cracked, and my jaw rattled and I'll tell you what I did believe in, remember oh most gracious, I believed in hope.

A lover may come back to you, after a wide circle of years, returning with questions in their hearts, with old hopes or with keys they stole. You will have a choice.

I've often wondered why most people refuse one another after the fallow years. Do they not know a circling love is an answer as well as a call?

There are things. There are always notes, sometimes written on bits of tape, inside of or underneath the objects she gives me. *These came from my father's house in Bray or My mother bought this set during the war at the Belfast market.*

The words mean more to me than the objects, and truthfully, her handwriting breaks my hard heart. Her handwriting is my way to claim her, makes her mine, makes her tangible.

And do you know something else? Every single time she leaves, somehow without my knowing, the copper and the silver have been polished to a shine. (They used to have to polish before the priest came, even the unseen pieces that stayed in the side table, because that is what one did.)

She knows that no priest will set foot in this house, and still, she polishes every single piece I own. And when I change the sheets on our beds, unearthed are her hidden rosaries.

It's like she wants me to be ready.

Last night, after I had urged you to go to bed, I wandered to the kitchen and found myself quite alone, my darling, quite alone.

These are the harsh nights, the crossroad nights, when I feel like a widow. I stood in the kitchen where we all used to gather. I buttered a piece of bread and cut two slices of cheese in the quiet of this memory house and felt quite lost and terrified, and I'll tell you why.

I can remember seeing my own mother stand this way, like an apparition or a soldier, with a piece of bread and cheese, quite alone and confused in the kitchen of our old house. Somehow, last night, we superimposed, she and I.

I had all these dreams, you see, of a house full of people, of a home. With dog and daddy gone, with your brother gone and you leaving in stages, I am emptied. I am the child who saw her mother alone in the kitchen, confronting something bigger than she could manage. I am the mother alone in the kitchen, accepting something smaller than she had planned.

I tried to make it just about hunger, simply about the bread and the cheese, but in the end, and always, it seems to be about

Do not be the first to break the circle
of an embrace.

Linger.

When my time drew near, she flew to be with me. By then, I was heavy, pulled toward the earth in a way that made me feel mortal like a tree.

Waiting for her suitcases, we sat down together. She held her flowers in one hand, and put her other hand on my belly. Her face lit up with joy, and I would even venture to say reverence.

I had never seen such a look for me.
It made me shy and glad.

I tell you, there was no space between us, no chasm, not one iota of distance. We were radiant joy three days before you were born. We were pure potential in that moment. Sitting there, the hive of movement around us, of the coming and going, of the greeting and departing, we were a still point, neither hesitation nor anticipation. I had joined her in the rank of mater, and the celebration was soon to start. The death of me was imminent too, and she knew this but couldn't tell me.

Never matter, why mourn when the celebration was soon to start? Because in that moment, in her face I saw that I could do no wrong. In that moment, I was born.

I wasn't one of those women who wanted to look in the mirror to see you coming. I can remember the midwives shouting Look, the baby is coming — but I kept my eyelids clamped together.

When you were born and they laid you on my chest, you didn't scream like in the movies. You sounded weary and relieved, as though you'd survived some reckless voyage at sea and crawled up on the shore, exhausted.

The midwives tended to you and I drank tea and ate toast with butter and jam. Everyone else slept. My body was all saltwater taffy, pulled and pendulous. The midwife helped me to the shower where I stood in full nudity, for once not caring about modesty. The water slid over the pulp of my beaten body, and this kindly woman, this seafaring woman stood and watched me, watched the blood pool at my feet and warned me about the milk coming in and did I have cool cabbage leaves at home?

I didn't.

You were perfect.

Acknowledgements

Thank you to my editor, Seán Virgo, who understood the spirit of this work. His deft and careful attention has permeated throughout. Thank you to my friend Kimberley French, for her generosity in permitting me to use her photograph for the cover, and for connecting me to Susan Musgrave. Kim, I am forever grateful to you. Both Susan Musgrave and Lorna Crozier, thank you for your mentorship, truly, and for guiding me through this process. Thanks to everyone at Thistledown Press for helping me make manifest this collection.

There were many early readers to whom I owe such deep gratitude: Lyndon Penner, Lina Di Gregorio, David Lee, Kim Gray, Melanie Jones , and Carmen Alger. Thanks also to Andy Moro and Tara Beagan for potlucks and plotting. Thank you to all the members of my writers' group: Heather Setka, Mikka Jacobsen, Richard Kemmick, Judith Pond, Shelley Youngblut, Lisa Balderassa, Russ Peters and Sonia Perna. Your reflections were invaluable, and your support immeasurable. To each of you, my thanks.

Most especially, I offer the deepest gratitude to my mother and to my daughter. Both are fierce warriors of the heart, and of the truth. My admiration and love knows no bounds.